BOOK TWO
A DOZEN A DAY
SONGBOOK

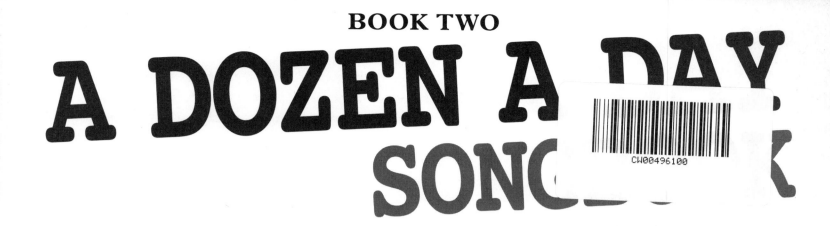

Pop Hits

**Including music from Katy Perry, ABBA,
Stevie Wonder, James Blunt plus many more...**

© Copyright 2013 The Willis Music Company
Florence, Kentucky, USA. All Rights Reserved.

Exclusive Distributors:
Music Sales Limited
Newmarket Road, Bury St Edmunds, Suffolk IP33 3YB, UK.
Music Sales Pty Limited
Units 3-4, 17 Willfox Street, Condell Park, NSW 2200, Australia.

Order No. WMR101233
ISBN: 978-1-78038-909-7

Unauthorised reproduction of any part of this publication by any means
including photocopying is an infringement of copyright.

Arrangements, engravings and audio supplied by Camden Music Services.
CD audio arranged, programmed and mixed by Jeremy Birchall and Christopher Hussey.
Edited by Sam Lung.
CD recorded, mixed and mastered by Jonas Persson.

Printed in the EU.

Your Guarantee of Quality
As publishers, we strive to produce every book to the highest commercial standards.
This book has been carefully designed to minimise awkward page turns and to make
playing from it a real pleasure. Particular care has been given to specifying acid-free,
neutral-sized paper made from pulps which have not been elemental chlorine bleached.
This pulp is from farmed sustainable forests and was produced with special regard for
the environment. Throughout, the printing and binding have been planned to ensure a
sturdy, attractive publication which should give years of enjoyment. If your copy fails to
meet our high standards, please inform us and we will gladly replace it.

www.musicsales.com

THE WILLIS MUSIC COMPANY

This collection of well-known pop pieces can be used on its own or as supplementary material to the iconic *A Dozen A Day* techniques series by Edna Mae Burnam. The pieces have been arranged to progress gradually, applying concepts and patterns from Burnam's technical exercises whenever possible. Suggested guidelines for use with the original series are also provided.

These arrangements are excellent supplements for any method and may also be used for sight-reading practice for more advanced students.

The difficulty titles of certain editions of the *A Dozen A Day* books may vary internationally. This repertoire book corresponds to the third difficulty level.

Contents

Someone Like You

Use with A Dozen A Day Book Two, after Group I (page 4)

TRACKS 1–2

Words & Music by Adele Adkins & Daniel Wilson
Arranged by Christopher Hussey

© Copyright 2010 Universal Music Publishing Limited/Sugar Lake Music/Chrysalis Music Limited.
All Rights Reserved. International Copyright Secured.

You Are The Sunshine Of My Life

Use after Group I (page 4)

Words & Music by Stevie Wonder
Arranged by Christopher Hussey

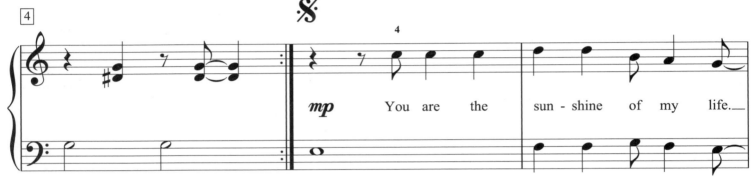

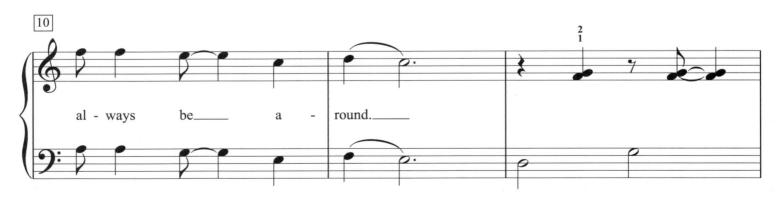

© Copyright 1972 Jobete Music Company Incorporated/Black Bull Music, USA.
Jobete Music (UK) Limited/Black Bull Music.
All Rights Reserved. International Copyright Secured.

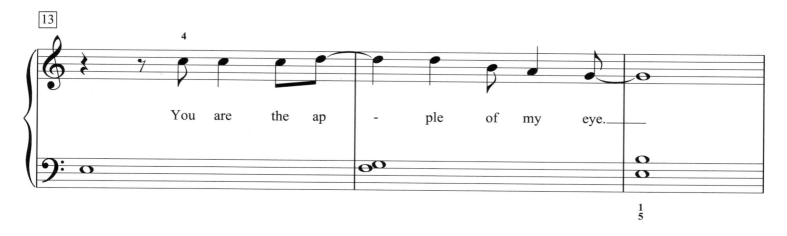

You are the ap - ple of my eye.

For - ev - er,____ you'll stay in____ my

To Coda ⊕

heart.____   𝆒   I feel like this____

____ is the be - gin - ning,____

though I've loved you___ for a mil - lion years.___

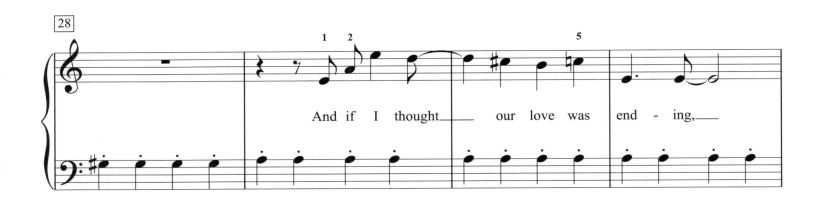

And if I thought___ our love was end - ing,___

I'd___ find my - self___ drown - ing in my___ own

D.S. al Coda $\oplus$ **CODA**

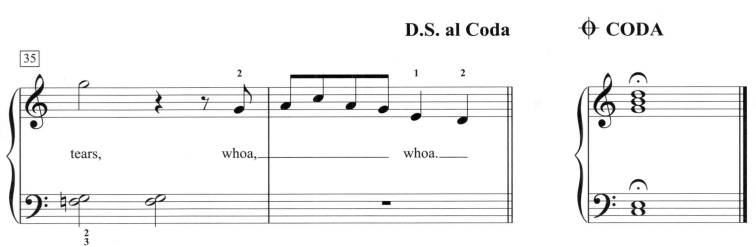

tears,   whoa,_____ whoa.___

My Life Would Suck Without You

Use after Group II (page 9)

TRACKS 5–6

Words & Music by Max Martin,
Lukasz Gottwald & Claude Kelly
Arranged by Christopher Hussey

With a drive

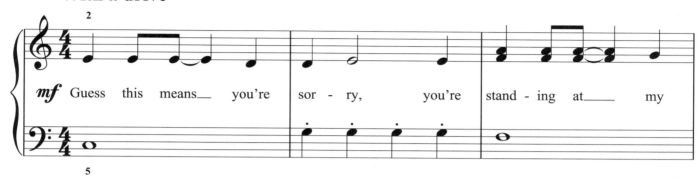

Guess this means___ you're sor - ry, you're stand - ing at___ my

door. Guess this means___ you take back

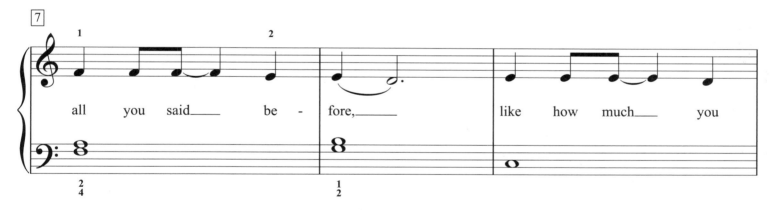

all you said___ be - fore,___ like how much___ you

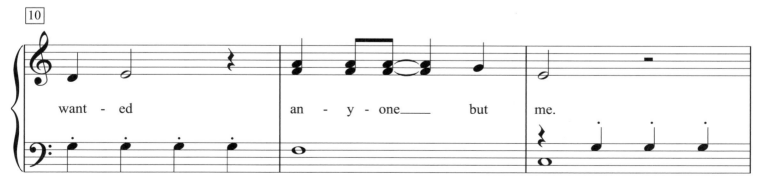

want - ed an - y - one___ but me.

© Copyright 2008 Maratone AB/Warner Tamerlane Publishing Corporation/Kasz Money Publishing/Studio Beast Music.
Kobalt Music Publishing Limited/Warner/Chappell North America Limited.
All Rights Reserved. International Copyright Secured.

Said you'd nev - er come back, but here you are_ a -

- gain._ *f* 'Cause we be - long_ to - geth -

- - er now,_ yeah, for - ev - er u - ni -

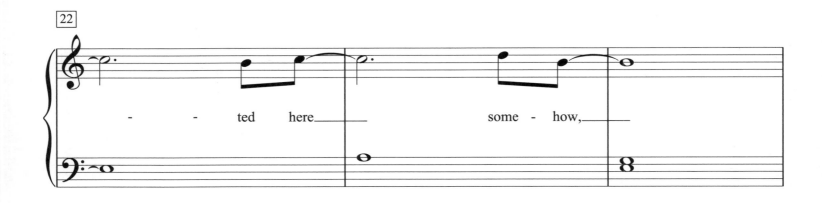

- - ted here_ some - how,_

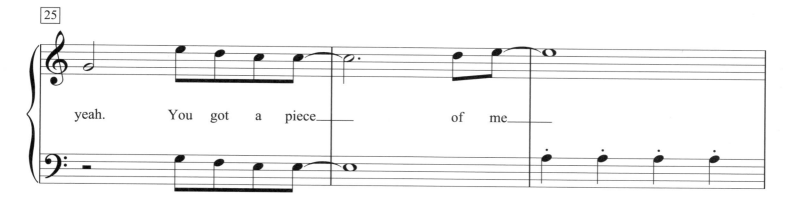

yeah. You got a piece___ of me___

and, hon - est - ly,___ my

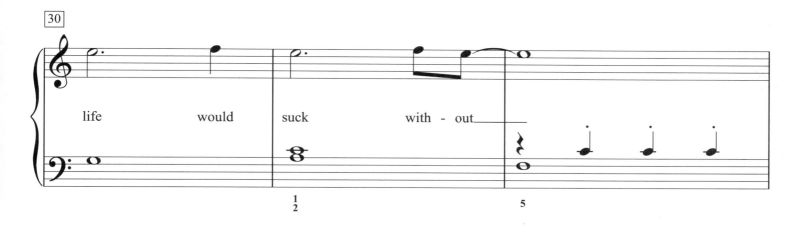

life would suck with - out___

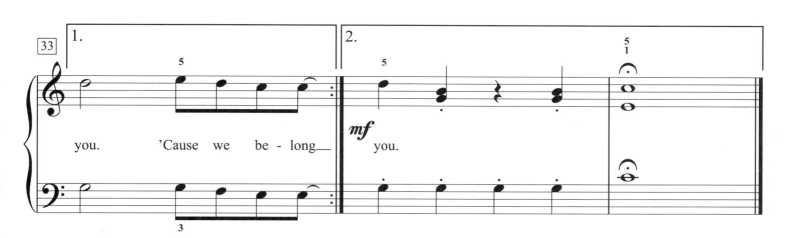

you. 'Cause we be - long___ you.

Patience

Use after Group II (page 9)

**TRACKS
7-8**

Words & Music by Mark Owen,
Gary Barlow, Jason Orange,
Howard Donald & John Shanks
Arranged by Christopher Hussey

Smoothly

© Copyright 2006 EMI Music Publishing Limited/Warner/Chappell North America Limited/
Universal Music Publishing MGB Limited/Sony/ATV Music Publishing.
All Rights Reserved. International Copyright Secured.

I Will Always Love You

Use after Group III (page 14)

TRACKS
9–10

Words & Music by Dolly Parton
Arranged by Christopher Hussey

© Copyright 1973 Velvet Apple Music, USA.

Carlin Music Corporation for the world (excluding Germany, Austria, Switzerland, Scandinavia, Eastern Europe, Australia, New Zealand, Japan, South Africa, Canada and the United States of America). All Rights Reserved. International Copyright Secured.

me._____ So, good - bye, please don't___ cry; we both

know I'm not what you, you need._____ *mf* And

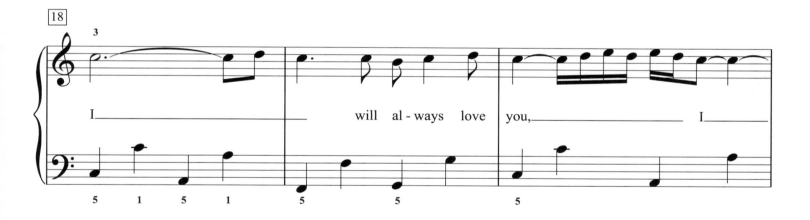

I_____ will al - ways love you,_____ I___

___ will al - ways love you._____

1-5

Bridge Over Troubled Water

Use after Group III (page 14)

Words & Music by Paul Simon
Arranged by Christopher Hussey

**TRACKS
11–12**

© Copyright 1969 Paul Simon (BMI).
All Rights Reserved. International Copyright Secured.

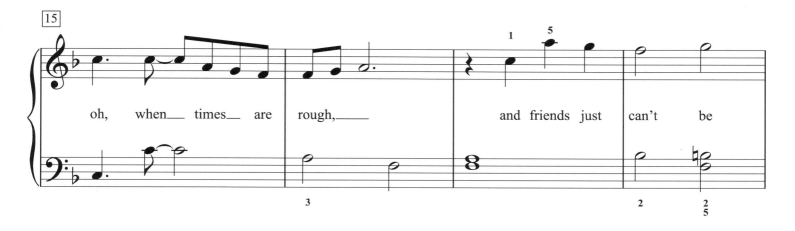

oh, when___ times___ are rough,___ and friends just can't be

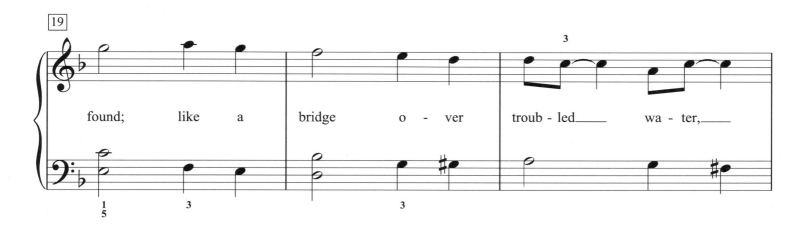

found; like a bridge o - ver troub - led___ wa - ter,___

I will lay me down.___ Like a bridge o - ver

troub - led___ wa - ter, I will lay me down.___

19

Can You Feel The Love Tonight

from Walt Disney Pictures' THE LION KING

Use after Group IV (page 20)

Words by Tim Rice
Music by Elton John
Arranged by Christopher Hussey

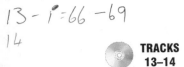

**TRACKS
13–14**

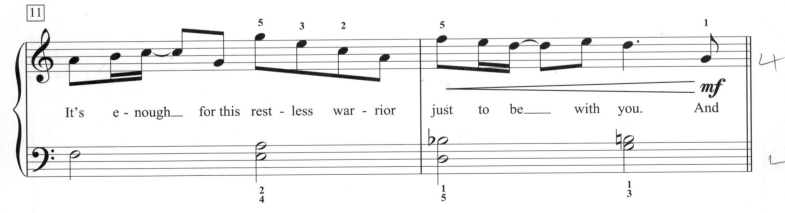

© Copyright 1994 Wonderland Music Company Incorporated, USA.
All Rights Reserved. International Copyright Secured.

Last Friday Night (T.G.I.F.)

Use after Group IV (page 20)

TRACKS
15–16

Words & Music by Max Martin,
Lukasz Gottwald, Bonnie McKee & Katy Perry
Arranged by Christopher Hussey

Confidently

© Copyright 2010 Maratone AB/Kasz Money Publishing/When I'm Rich You'll Be My Bitch/Where Da Kasz At/Prescription Songs LLC/Bonnie McKee Music.
Kassner Associated Music Publishers Limited/Kobalt Music Publishing Limited/Warner/Chappell North America Limited.
All Rights Reserved. International Copyright Secured.

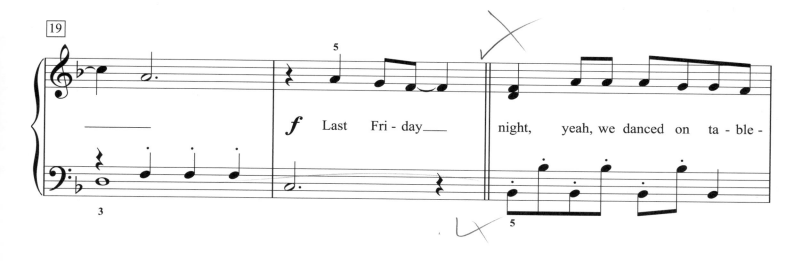

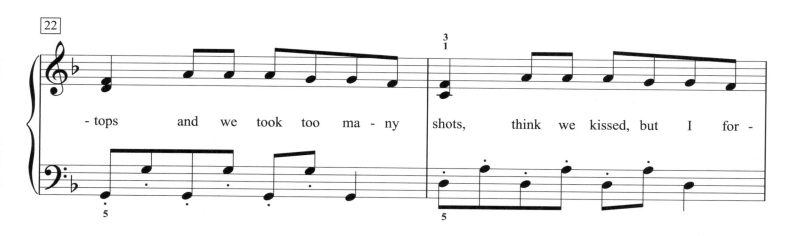

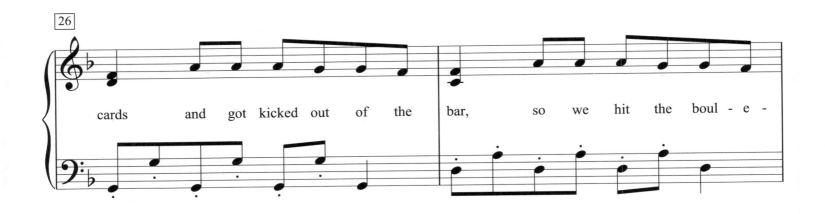

night, yeah, I think we broke the law, al - ways say we're gon - na

sto - op,___ oo, oh.___ This Fri - day___ night, do it all___

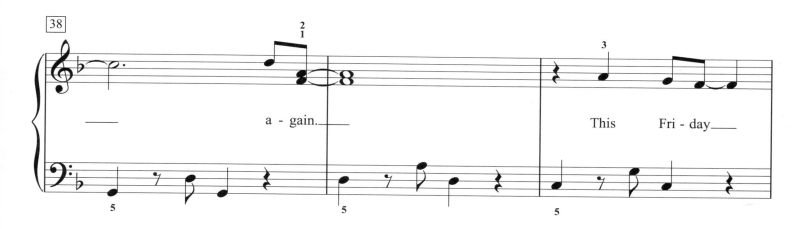

___ a - gain.___ This Fri - day___

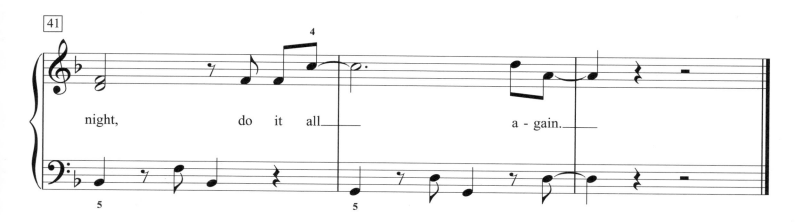

night, do it all___ a - gain.___

You're Beautiful

Use after Group V (page 28)

TRACKS
17–18

Words & Music by Sacha Skarbek,
James Blunt & Amanda Ghost
Arranged by Christopher Hussey

© Copyright 2004 EMI Music Publishing Limited/Bucks Music Group Limited.
All Rights Reserved. International Copyright Secured.

Dancing Queen

Use after Group V (page 28)

TRACKS 19–20

Words & Music by Benny Andersson,
Stig Anderson & Björn Ulvaeus
Arranged by Christopher Hussey

© Copyright 1976 Union Songs AB, Sweden.
Bocu Music Limited for Great Britain and the Republic Of Ireland. All rights in Germany administered by Universal Music Publ. GmbH.
All Rights Reserved. International Copyright Secured.

A DOZEN A DAY
SONGBOOK

Complete the whole series!

These songbooks feature fantastic collections of timeless classical and pop pieces, arranged for piano and accompanied with fully-orchestrated audio CDs. They can be enjoyed on their own or as supplementary material to the iconic *A Dozen A Day* technique series by Edna Mae Burnam.